T0109162

The Naturally
Bug-Free Garden

The Naturally Bug-

Free Garden

Controlling Pest Insects without Chemicals

Anna Hess

Skyhorse Publishing

First Skyhorse paperback edition 2015

Skyhorse Publishing books may be purchased in bulk at special discounts for sales promotion, corporate gifts, fund-raising, or educational purposes. Special editions can also be created to specifications. For details, contact the Special Sales Department, Skyhorse Publishing, 307 West 36th Street, 11th Floor, New York, NY 10018 or info@skyhorsepublishing.com.

Skyhorse® and Skyhorse Publishing® are registered trademarks of Skyhorse Publishing, Inc.®, a Delaware corporation.

Visit our website at www.skyhorsepublishing.com.

10 9 8 7 6 5 4 3

Library of Congress Cataloging-in-Publication Data is available on file.

Cover design by KissCut Designs

Print ISBN: 978-1-63220-630-5

Printed in China

Table of Contents

Introduction

Many leaf nibblers, like this bush katydid (*Scudderia* sp.), are solitary and go largely unnoticed in the garden.

Insects are one of the most serious problems facing many organic fruit and vegetable growers, and I was certainly no exception at the beginning of my homesteading career. For the last eight years, my husband and I have grown most of our own food, and some days I was ready to throw in the towel. Our squash plants melted into puddles of wilted leaves just before they set fruit (vine borers at work), tiny grubs defoliated our asparagus fronds (asparagus beetles chowing down), and mysterious insects arrived in the night to eat our Swiss-chard leaves (striped blister beetles being bad). Our broccoli was so covered in cabbageworms that it seemed easier to toss the food than to eat it, and Japanese beetles dripped from our grapevines.

Our neighbors told us to spray, but even seemingly safe pesticides like Bt and neem oil gave me the willies. Wasn't there a way to grow our food without any chemical inputs at all?

The answer was yes, but only once we learned to bend a little to nature's whims. A garden ecosystem is always going to be at least slightly out of balance because humans have manipulated the soil and landscape to promote productivity, but we can still do our best to bring natural forces to bear against insect pests. My husband and I beat squash vine borers with variety selection and succession planting, we waited for natural predators to defeat the asparagus and blister beetles, we learned to plant our broccoli at a time when cabbage moths were dormant, and we switched over to a variety of grape that Japanese beetles don't enjoy. With these and other techniques, we eventually learned to keep pest insects in check without spraying anything at all. Using the tips in this book, you can do the same in your own garden!

(As a final side note before you delve into the meat of natural insect control, I wanted to alert you to the presence of a glossary in the back of this book. Now and then I'll use a term like "permaculture" or "Bt" and will assume you know what I'm talking about. If you do—great! If not, just flip to the glossary for a quick refresher course on these advanced homesteading topics.)

What Is a Naturally Bug-Free Garden?

A praying mantis moved into a bed of buggy beans in search of a high-protein snack.

Is a naturally bug-free garden a spot where no creepy crawlies of any sort reside? Far from it! In fact, if you follow my lead and use the bug-control methods outlined in this book, you'll soon be seeing bees on your squash flowers and mantises in your beans. Beneficials (the good bugs) will be everywhere.

And your garden won't even *really* be free of pest invertebrates. It's necessary to keep the bad guys around in low numbers in order to attract the good guys, so you'll still see the occasional slug and cucumber beetle. On the other hand, you'll no longer find plants so overcome by the bad bugs that they can't hold their heads up high, so you might stop noticing the pests entirely as nature takes over the job of keeping bad-bug populations in check.

When it comes right down to it, the only thing a naturally bug-free garden is really free of is the gardener's need to wage war against pests. It's the *gardener*, not the garden, who is set free. And that freedom is what we were really looking for all along, isn't it?

PART

The Garden Ecosystem

The presence of centipedes and other predators is a sign your garden is in balance.

Chapter 1: Identifying Your Bugs

I was concerned when I first noticed these dark scales on dead asparagus stalks, but I soon realized they were simply the eggs of the innocuous katydid that sings me to sleep on autumn nights.

Many new gardeners assume that every bug is a bad bug, but the truth is that a significant number of the creepy crawlies you'll find on your vegetables are either random passersby, beneficial pollinators, or predators of leaf nibblers. The trick is to know the difference, and to understand how larger animals fit into the complex web of garden life.

Since it's so easy to mistake good bugs for bad bugs, my first rule when dealing with garden insects is to identify everything I see. *The Naturally Bug-Free Garden* is too short to introduce every garden character, but this chapter will at least give you a frame of reference for identifying unknown bugs, along with some key identification resources. Between the identification tips found here and the profiles in later chapters of common garden friends and foes, you should soon be able to put a name to most critters that show up in your yard.

Types of Invertebrates

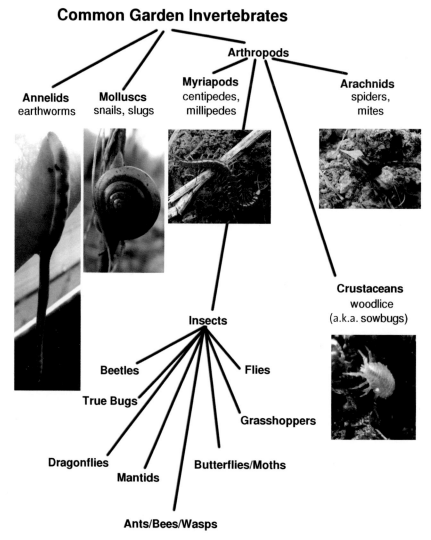

Common Garden Invertebrates

Arthropods

Annelids
earthworms

Molluscs
snails, slugs

Myriapods
centipedes,
millipedes

Arachnids
spiders,
mites

Crustaceans
woodlice
(a.k.a. sowbugs)

Insects

Beetles

Flies

True Bugs

Grasshoppers

Dragonflies

Mantids

Butterflies/Moths

Ants/Bees/Wasps

The most common types of invertebrates visible to the naked eye in a garden are annelids (worms), molluscs (snails and slugs), myriapods (centipedes and millipedes), arachnids (spiders and mites), crustaceans (woodlice and crayfish), and insects.

Your first step when you find an unknown bug should be to figure out which large categories the animal fits into. Starting at the top, nearly all garden bugs are known as invertebrates because they have no backbone. (I incorrectly call them "bugs" throughout this book when I'm not feeling very scientific.)

The chart on the previous page shows the wide range of invertebrates you can find in most backyards. The major categories include annelids (worms), mollusks (snails and slugs), myriapods (centipedes and millipedes), arachnids (spiders and mites), crustaceans (woodlice and crayfish), and insects. Among insects, the most common categories are beetles (with hard wing covers), flies (with only one pair of flight wings, the other wing pair having been reduced to knobs), true bugs (with sucking mouthparts and including cicadas, aphids, leafhoppers, and shield bugs), grasshoppers and their kin (including crickets and katydids), butterflies and moths (and the caterpillars that are their larvae), hymenoptera (ants, bees, and wasps), and dragonflies (along with the related damselflies). If you can tell these major groups of insects apart, you'll be well on your way to identifying the next unknown bug in your garden.

It's handy to be familiar with each stage of an insect's life cycle. The photos here all show Mexican bean beetles: eggs, a larva, and an adult.

Identification Resources

When I find an unknown denizen of the garden, I usually start my identification campaign with the Internet. If you go to www.images.google.com and type in some identifying features, your pest's mug shot may pop right up. For example, when I saw my first asparagus beetles, I typed in "orange beetle on asparagus," and the species I was looking for turned up in the first row of search results. You'll notice that a good search often includes the category of invertebrate, its color, and the plant the bug is found on.

If a simple image search fails, I turn to books next. *Garden Insects of North America* by Whitney Cranshaw is my favorite invertebrate field guide because its full-color photos usually help me narrow down my search quickly. Several other field guides to garden insects (or just to insects in general) also exist, and any of these titles can help you identify your garden friends and foes.

Earthworms are one of the classic beneficial invertebrates.

But sometimes books fail me as well. At that point, I usually turn to www.bugguide.net, which is the Wikipedia of the invertebrate world. I can often identify an invertebrate (or at least get close) by working my way through BugGuide's key, but if I'm thoroughly stumped, I will log in to the site and submit a photo, requesting identification help. One of the volunteers gets back to me within a day or two, telling me which species (or category) of invertebrate I've found. Those of you less technologically inclined may get the same results by capturing the questionable insect in a jar and taking it to your local agricultural extension agent for identification. (Visit www.csrees.usda.gov/Extension/ to find the closest extension agent to you.)

No matter which method of identification you end up using, I urge you not to skip this step! I focused on insect identification first for a reason—you can't work to promote the good bugs and minimize the bad bugs if you can't tell them apart.

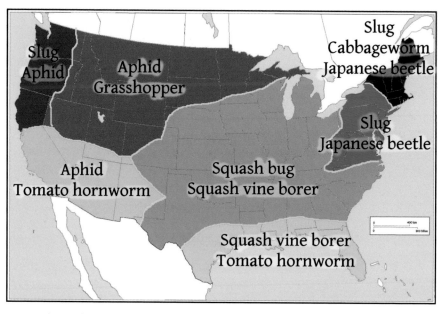

A survey by *Mother Earth News* showed that home gardeners' worst pests varied by location.

Chapter 2:
Worst Garden Pests

Although you probably won't be able to identify every single invertebrate in your garden anytime soon, it's worth knowing the worst offenders on sight. To that end, this chapter includes a brief rundown of the natural history and common treatment methods for the twelve worst pests in home gardens (based on a *Mother Earth News* survey of 1,300 gardeners). As you read, please keep in mind that many of the mainstream organic treatments mentioned in this chapter aren't quite as kind to the earth as a permaculture gardener might like. I'll suggest alternatives later in the text, and you can also check the glossary for more information about the potential dangers of chemicals mentioned here.

Aphids

Aphids are often found in large colonies being tended by ants. The aphids benefit from predator protection, while the ants are allowed to consume excess plant sap that shoots through the aphids' system before it can be digested.

Aphids include many species of tiny insects that suck the juices out of plants. I find it interesting that aphids rank number three on *Mother Earth News*'s survey of worst garden pests because, in my own garden, the tiny critters only show up when I'm guilty of over-fertilization. Even then, aphids are quickly wiped out by natural predators.

Mother Earth News gardeners treat aphids by pruning off infected plant parts, by attracting beneficial insects, and by applying insecticidal soap. I recommend first lowering the nitrogen content of your fertilization campaign, then ensuring that you have plenty of natural predators to go around.

Who are these natural predators that do such a good job of controlling aphids? Ladybugs are the best-known of the common aphid eaters, but tiny wasps will also show up to parasitize the problematic juice suckers, and lacewing larvae, minute pirate bugs, hoverfly larvae, big-eyed bugs, damsel bugs, and the larvae of predatory midges feed on aphids too. Letting aphid populations thrive unchecked will attract many of these predators, the flowers I list in Chapter 3 will boost the populations of other predators, and a shallow water source like a bird bath full of stones will bring predatory midges to your yard.

Cabbageworms

The most common species of cabbageworm is the larva of the cabbage white (*Pieris rapae*), sometimes confusingly called a "cabbage moth" even though it is really a type of butterfly.

The southern cabbageworm is the larva of the related checkered white (*Pontia protodice*), which is found primarily in the southern United States. A few other caterpillars are also sometimes called cabbageworms.

Cabbageworms come in multiple species, but most of you will only run across the two most common types mentioned here. The green caterpillar of the cabbage white is the most widespread nibbler on crucifer leaves, and I find this cabbageworm easy to control by handpicking in my own garden. Southern cabbageworms are much harder to manage since the spotted caterpillars tend to live inside the florets of broccoli plants, where the caterpillars are inaccessible until after harvest.

Mother Earth News gardeners have reported luck with control strategies that include Bt, spinosad, row covers, and promoting caterpillar predators (such as paper wasps and yellow jackets). Timing seems to be relatively effective in my garden, since the cabbageworms are killed (or at least slowed down) by frosts in the late fall and early spring. If we can get our broccoli and cabbage sets out into the garden early enough in the spring, we see little damage before harvest; similarly, a late-fall planting also misses the peak cabbageworm season. With cabbageworm populations minimized due to careful crop timing, I'm able to round out my control campaign with variety selection (Chapter 7) and handpicking (Chapter 8).

Corn Earworms

Photo credit: Ruth Hazzard, University of Massachusetts.

Corn earworms are largely a cosmetic problem in the home garden.

Corn earthworms (*Helicoverpa zea*) are caterpillars that tunnel into the ends of ears of corn, as well as into tomatoes and a few other crops. Despite being on the *Mother Earth News* top-pest list, I consider earworms to be only a cosmetic problem in our garden. Most of our ears of corn never get damaged, and it's easy to break off the affected portion on those that do.

If you can't stand blemished vegetables, though, you can prevent earworm damage by applying vegetable oil or Bt to the tips of ears when silks start to show, or by planting varieties with tight ear tips. (See Chapter 7 for more information on resistant vegetable varieties.)

Cucumber Beetles

Cucumber beetles include two species: striped cucumber beetles (*Acalymma vittata*) and spotted cucumber beetles (*Diabrotica undecimpunctata howardi*). Both feed on melon and cucumber plants, transferring a bacterial disease known as wilt to the vegetables. Bacterial wilt symptoms begin with drooping of the leaves, followed by death of the plant. For a definitive diagnosis, cut the cucurbit's stem and squeeze the cut ends—if the plant has succumbed to bacterial wilt, a sticky sap will ooze out and will form a long thread when you touch the two cut ends back together and then slowly pull them apart again.

Cucumber beetles are problematic because they carry bacterial wilt disease.

Mother Earth News gardeners recommend handpicking cucumber beetles, treating with neem oil, cleaning up the garden to prevent overwintering locations, and utilizing poultry, row covers, companion planting, and yellow sticky traps. I simply succession plant my cucumbers (Chapter 6), don't plant cantaloupes, and choose resistant varieties of both cucumbers and watermelons (Chapter 7).

Cutworms

Cutworms are caterpillars that live in the soil and feed on young plants. Their pupae are often found in the soil in the spring.

Cutworms are often invisible in the garden since they live in the soil, but you'll know you have these pesky caterpillars if your seedlings are beheaded in the night. Cutworms belong to any of several species of moths, but the most common type in North American gardens is the variegated cutworm (*Peridroma saucia*). *Mother Earth News* gardeners recommend making little collars around the bases of seedlings to protect them from damage, cultivating soil before planting, or setting out larger

Herrick Kimball, author of *The Planet Whizbang Idea Book for Gardeners*, uses split goldenrod stems to protect seedlings from cutworms.

seedlings. Natural predators seem to keep cutworms under control in our garden during most years, and I always germinate enough seedlings that I can replace any transplants that get eaten in the night.

Grasshoppers

Grasshoppers include a number of species that eat leaves, but that are rarely a problem in the vegetable garden. Most pest grasshoppers are members of the genus *Melanoplus*, including two-striped grasshoppers (*M. bivittatus*), differential grasshoppers (*M. differentialis*), migratory grasshoppers (*M. sanguinipes*), and red-legged grasshoppers (*M. femurrubrum*). Besides eating grass, grasshoppers enjoy the leaves of beans, leafy greens, and corn. *Mother Earth News* gardeners treat grasshopper infestations with hungry chickens and guinea fowl while I rely on natural garden predators to keep grasshopper populations under control.

A grasshopper sheds its tough skin like a snake does, allowing the insect to grow larger.

Japanese Beetles

Japanese beetles (*Popillia japonica*) are iridescent insects that come out of the ground for a couple of months in the summer, during which time they can completely defoliate their favorite plants (especially roses, grapes, and cherries). During the rest of the year, Japanese beetles live as white grubs in the soil, where the larval beetles do some damage feeding on plant roots.

My primary method of controlling these invasive beetles is handpicking the adult insects (Chapter 8), along with choosing plant species

Japanese beetles often congregate in clusters as males compete to mate with a female.

and varieties that are a less attractive source of food (which I'll explain in more depth in Chapter 7). *Mother Earth News* gardeners add the use of trap crops, chickens, guinea fowl, ducks, robins, and bluebirds. In particular, they recommend letting birds work over the ground in late spring when beetle larvae are close to the surface and can be easily scratched up.

One seemingly innovative approach to Japanese-beetle control is to use purchased pheromones to attract Japanese beetles toward sticky traps in the spring. Some gardeners even go so far as to put the lures above a funnel that feeds into a PVC pipe and drops the crunchy treats into a cup of water at chicken eye level. Unfortunately, the home gardener should be aware that studies of the efficacy of these traps show that the pheromone not only attracts the beetles that come out of your soil, but the scent also brings in all of your neighbors' bugs as well. Since many of the attracted Japanese beetles settle onto plants around the trap rather than being captured by the sticky paper or chicken funnel, gardeners who use Japanese-beetle lures usually see higher, rather than lower, populations of these troublesome insects in their yards. I guess the lures aren't such a good idea for the home gardener after all.

Slugs

Slugs thrive in damp climates and tend to multiply in gardens topped with a heavy coating of mulch.

Slugs (and their shelled relatives, snails) tend to top the list of problematic pests in areas that stay cool and damp during the summer, especially among gardeners who use heavy mulches. However, you shouldn't jump to the conclusion that any mollusk you find in the garden is bad news. Unlike many of the pests mentioned in this chapter, the term "slug" is a very general one, and saying "slugs are bad for gardens" is a lot like saying "birds are bad for gardens." While it's true that many slugs chew on leaves, others are decomposers that break down the dead plant matter on the soil surface (like your straw mulch), while a few even eat other slugs.

How can you tell the difference between the good slugs and the bad slugs? I generally consider any invertebrate in the garden to be good until I'm proven wrong, which in a slug's case consists of catching the mollusk in the act of eating my lettuce or strawberries. If you want to learn slug identification, the worst slugs include the milky garden slug (*Deroceras reticulatum*), the midget milky garden slug (*Deroceras agreste*), the marsh slug (*Deroceras laeve*), the great gray garden slug (*Limax maximus*), and the tawny garden slug (*Limax flavus*). Those of you living in the Pacific Northwest will be relieved to hear that the banana slug (*Ariolimax* spp.) is not a garden pest.

Mother Earth News readers report good luck with slug-control methods including handpicking, iron-phosphate baits, diatomaceous earth, beer traps, chickens, garter snakes, and ducks. (More on ducks in Chapter 4—the poultry aren't always as well-behaved in the garden as some books suggest.) My recommendation? Don't till. Cultivating soil tends to kill natural predators of slugs (like toads, salamanders, and snakes), and if you devastate the predator population, mulching will soon result in a garden overrun with slimy nibblers. However, if you don't churn up your soil, mollusks' natural enemies provide quite adequate slug control. I live in an area that averages a full inch of rain per week, much of my garden is located in partial shade, and our groundwater is very high, so our garden stays pretty soppy. But slugs are only a minor problem amid our vegetables because we work hard to promote predator populations and we never till the ground. My conclusion is that, if you live in a slug-friendly part of the country, you should either till and don't mulch or, better, mulch and don't till.

Squash Bugs

Squash bugs (*Anasa tristis*) suck the juices out of the leaves of cucurbits (especially pumpkins and squash), causing them to wilt. Handpicking is a particularly effective method of squash-bug control, especially if you catch the insects at the egg stage. In addition, placing boards on the ground beside your squash plants provides a nighttime hiding place for adult squash bugs, which are easy to crush the next morning. *Mother Earth News* readers also recommend cleaning up infested plants, applying

Squash bug adults look a bit like stink bugs. Their eggs are found in V-shaped clusters between plant veins, where the eggs hatch into greenish larvae that later turn pale gray.

neem oil to egg clusters and juvenile bugs, protecting plants with row covers, and utilizing late planting. In my own garden, I simply plant resistant varieties (see Chapter 7), especially butternuts. Finally, one of my readers recommends using ragweed to attract praying mantises that in turn eat the problematic squash bugs. See Chapter 3 for more on the ragweed version of squash-bug control.

Squash Vine Borers

Squash vine borers can be hard to see, but an infestation is evident when squash plants collapse overnight.

Squash vine borers (*Melitta cucurbitae*) are often identified by their symptoms rather than by spotting the insects themselves. A happy squash plant will suddenly wilt and then perish even though water is abundant, proving that vine borers have eaten their way through the stem. I'll discuss my methods for controlling this pesky insect in Chapters 6 and 7, so here I'll just list *Mother Earth News* gardeners' treatments: crop rotation, resistant varieties, mounding dirt over stems to promote rooting at nodes, and late planting.

Tomato and Tobacco Hornworms

Tomato hornworms (*Manduca quinquemaculata*) and tobacco hornworms (*Manduca sexta*) are large, green caterpillars that eat the leaves of tomato plants before transforming into hummingbird-like sphinx moths. As you can see from the white sacs in the photo on the next page, our hornworm problem is always controlled quickly by braconid wasps, which lay their eggs just under the skin of the caterpillar. The baby wasps feed on the body of the hornworm, then the parasitoids push their way to the outside of their host to spin cocoons. After transforming into adults within their cocoons, the wasps chew their way free so they can mate and lay eggs on more caterpillars. If you see hornworms similarly parasitized, leave them alone and the tiny wasps will soon spread throughout your garden.

White cocoons on this hornworm are a sign that the caterpillar has been eaten alive from the inside out by parasitoid wasps.

Along with encouraging braconid wasps, *Mother Earth News* gardeners use handpicking and Bt to control tomato and tobacco hornworms. In addition, a recent study suggests that tomato plants are able to respond to the chewing action of hornworms by creating compounds in their leaves that will kill up to a third of future munchers—see Chapter 5 for more information on this type of plant defense. In other words, it's quite possible that even if you see hornworms in your garden, the pests are nothing to worry about since the garden ecosystem already has the problem well in hand.

Whiteflies

Whiteflies (*Trialeurodes vaporariorum* and related species) are tiny, winged insects that suck the juices out of plants, much like aphids do. Like aphids, I never have problems with whiteflies unless I've blocked out their natural predators, such as when I grow fall greens under quick hoops or when I take houseplants inside over the winter. *Mother Earth News* gardeners treat whiteflies with insecticidal soaps, but I generally just wait until I'm able to put the houseplants outside, allowing natural predators to demolish pest populations. Since whiteflies can't stand freezing temperatures, you can also uncover moderately hardy garden plants during light freezes to devastate whitefly

Whiteflies are usually found on houseplants and in greenhouses.

infestations. If your climate is too warm to freeze whiteflies out, then be sure to keep your plants uncovered so natural predators can take care of the problem.

Other Bad Bugs

In addition to this dirty dozen of problematic insects, runners-up include: Mexican bean beetles (*Epilachna varivestis*, discussed in Chapter 7), Colorado potato beetles (*Leptinotarsa decemlineata*), flea beetles (several species in subfamily Alticinae, discussed in Chapter 7), and asparagus beetles (*Crioceris asparagi*, discussed in Chapter 5). And then there are the insects that many gardeners consider pests, but that don't actually prey on your plants. For example, yellow jackets may sting you, but these wasps are actually beneficial insects in the garden since they eat large quantities of caterpillars and other bad bugs. I'm not going to cover "pests" that are only bad because they bother humans, but I will touch on other problematic insects later in this book. In addition, you'll also want to keep your eyes open and watch who chews on your leaves and who visits your flowers since each garden has its own unique array of problematic insects and beneficials. Your yard may be home to a species I don't even mention here, but chances are good that one of the control techniques I suggest will wipe out your bad bugs as well as it does mine.

Soldier beetle larvae act a bit like bad bugs in our garden since they like to suck sugar water out of fruits. But these insects are generally beneficial because they also suck the juices out of cucumber beetles, caterpillars, grasshopper eggs, and aphids.

Chapter 3:
The Good Bugs

After figuring out who the bad bugs are, your next goal in the garden should be to promote beneficial insects. But how can you tell which invertebrates are doing good work? I'm tempted to say that any bug who isn't obviously bad is a garden ally, but you should work especially hard to protect invertebrates who improve your soil, pollinate your crops, and control problematic insects. The sections that follow will give you a quick introduction to beneficials in each of these categories.

Soil Workers

This redworm is more likely to be found in decomposing horse manure or in a worm bin than in garden soil.

Nearly every invertebrate you find in the soil is a good bug with a job to do. Some (like earthworms and woodlice) digest organic matter and help build humus, while others (like centipedes and spiders) are busy eating smaller soil organisms. The combination of critters is essential for preventing the buildup of dead material on top of the soil and for releasing nutrients that plants use to grow.

On the other hand, a few soil critters are neutral or are actively bad for your garden. Ants can help disperse seeds of native plants, but they also protect aphids that suck the juices out of your trees and vegetables. Some grubs turn into Japanese beetles or June bugs (*Cotinus nitida*), the first of which eat the leaves of many fruit plants and the second of which enjoy consuming the fruits themselves. And then there are the cutworms I mentioned in the last chapter—plump caterpillars who nibble the tops off seedlings.

But even problematic soil inhabitants tend to loosen the soil and to carry organic matter deep beneath the surface. Earthworms—everyone's favorite denizen of the dirt—can eat their way ten feet deep, adding nutritious calcium to everything that passes through their gut. Ants are pretty useful in this respect too since they carry food down into their nests, resulting in pockets of rich soil, while bringing mineral-rich

A crawdad chimney is a sign that a crayfish is living in the groundwater under your garden. This type of soggy soil is best mounded up into raised beds to prevent waterlogging of plant roots.

subsoil to the surface. In wet areas (like my garden), crayfish do a similar job of nutrient movement.

Meanwhile, other organisms like those troublesome beetle grubs I mentioned previously fluff up soil and deposit nutrients in the form of their feces as they travel up and down through the earth. Ground-nesting bees and wasps such as sweat bees (*Halictus* sp.), miner bees (*Andrena* sp.), and various digger wasps all excavate burrows for their larvae to live in, while dung beetles fill their underground dens with rich balls of excrement. Of course, the bees, wasps, and dung beetles are all unequivocally good bugs since the first two pollinate your garden and often eat bad bugs, while the last help cycle nutrients through the ecosystem.

If you'd like a closer look at the critters who live beneath the surface, I recommend *Life in the Soil*, by James B. Nardi. On the other hand, if you just want to keep your garden healthy, it's pretty simple to promote life in the earth. Most soil organisms need damp ground, so topping your garden off with mulch is a great way to keep the critters active during hot summers. The use of cover crops and compost is also recommended since both will jumpstart your soil ecosystem by providing a buffet for microorganisms and invertebrates—think of compost and decomposing cover crops as bird feeders for the tiny inhabitants of your dirt.

What *shouldn't* you do to your soil? While tilling can break some pest-bug cycles, the practice also demolishes populations of beneficial soil organisms like earthworms. Chemical fertilizers have a similar effect, as does leaving the earth bare of plants or mulch so that erosion and heat can remove nutrients from the soil.

Why not nurture an organic, no-till garden and let your soil workers do the job of tilling and fertilizing for you? (I explain how to begin and maintain a no-till garden in *The Weekend Homesteader*.) Then you'll have a healthier garden and tastier vegetables . . . and won't have to work as hard!

Invasive but Beneficial

Pill bugs and sow bugs (also known as woodlice) are common residents of the compost pile. Most of the woodlice species found in the United States were introduced from Europe.

The average gardener doesn't realize that many of the invertebrates living in our soil and compost piles aren't native to the United States. All of the common woodlouse species in garden habitats (including pill bugs and sow bugs) were accidentally introduced from Europe, while the same is true of many of our earthworms and compost worms. As an environmentally-friendly gardener, should you be alarmed?

In most cases, the answer is no. However, it's worth taking a few steps to protect the native habitats around your garden. Invasive pill bugs don't seem to wander into the woods, but earthworms do, with devastating effects in forests far enough north that glaciation wiped out native earthworm species thousands of years ago. Since their introduction north of the glaciation line, invasive earthworms have changed soil dynamics by eating up the duff (leaf litter) on the forest floor, which in turn has affected the trees and wildflowers that grow in those northern forests.

Even in areas home to native earthworms, invasives tend to gain a foothold in disturbed and fragmented woodlands. Scientists

(continued)

(continued)

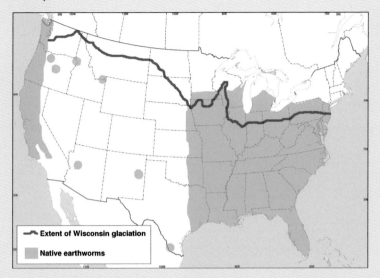

Extent of Wisconsin glaciation

Native earthworms

Native earthworms live primarily in the parts of the United States that weren't affected by the most recent glaciation. However, some worms have spread north into previously glaciated territory.

are beginning to realize that invasive earthworms in the South may be linked to the spread of invasive plants like the extremely troublesome Japanese stiltgrass, and that invasive worms might also compete with our forest salamanders.

What can you do to prevent these forest woes from getting worse? If you fish, never dump excess bait worms in the wild, and if you own a vermicomposting operation, steer clear of the highly invasive *Lumbricus rubellus*, a worm that can be identified by the lack of stripes between segments and by the presence of a yellow underside. (The more common *Eisenia fetida*, with yellowish stripes between segments, isn't a native species either, but doesn't seem to cause problems in the wild.) If you live north of the glaciation line and near native woodland, you should also be very careful when moving soil around so that you don't introduce invasive earthworms into areas where they're now absent.

With those steps in place, even invasive woodlice and earthworms can be a boon to your garden. The former work hard to turn your compost pile while the latter do the same in your soil. As long as they stay out of the woods, these soil invasives remain on the list of good garden invertebrates, at least in my book.

Pollinators

Even beetles can be pollinators, as I discovered when I went out to check on the first spring flowers in the woods. In the garden, beetles are most likely to pollinate low-sugar flowers like those on pear trees, where the beetles also gnaw holes in the petals. As a result of the flower damage, beetles are considered "mess and soil pollinators," beneficial in the edible garden but unsightly among ornamentals.

While soil workers may be the most essential invertebrates in your garden, the flashiest good bugs are pollinators. Honeybees (*Apis* sp.) are the poster children for pollination since they produce delicious honey as well as moving pollen from flower to flower, but you can have a very well-pollinated garden without building an apiary. In fact, some scientists believe that an overabundance of non-native honeybees causes declines in native-pollinator populations.

If you want to identify the insects visiting your flowers, I highly recommend the Xerces Society's beautifully illustrated book titled *Attracting Native Pollinators*. However, you don't really need to get so fancy as to figure out the species of each little insect on your apple blossoms in the spring. Nearly any bug on a flower is looking for pollen or nectar, and the pollen-hunter is likely to accidentally move pollen to the next flower in the process. Your goal should simply be to promote a diverse array of different pollinators in the garden throughout the year.

How will you know if your pollinator population *isn't* up to par? If you find cucumbers fat at one end and skinny at the other, baby summer squash that are rotting at the blossom end, blackberries with only a few plump lobes, or lopsided apples with a big side and a little side, your garden isn't seeing proper pollination. In some cases, inadequate pollination can be due to bad weather during bloom time, but if you notice problems, your first step should be to ensure that you're providing the proper habitat for wild pol-

Some insects you're probably already familiar with, like bumblebees, sweat bees (shown here), and carpenter bees, are high-quality pollinators.

len movers. (There's not much you can do about a cold spring.)

Attracting native pollinators can be nearly as simple as keeping your soil invertebrates happy. First, make sure you have wild or cultivated flowers blooming for as much of the year as possible, and remember that tiny bees may fly only 600 feet or less each day in search of food. The Xerces Society recommends big patches of flowers at least three feet in diameter so the clumps are easy for insects to see during their aerial commute, with smaller rows of flowers tempting the pollinators to continue their explorations out into your garden. The goal is to tempt a healthy population of pollinators into taking up residence on your homestead so they're raring to go when your fruit trees bloom in the spring and your cucumber flowers unfurl in the summer, needing their services.

Allowing clover and other weeds to grow in your lawn will keep the bees happy.

THE GARDEN ECOSYSTEM

Virgin's bower and other wild plants will feed pollinators like this honeybee if you allow the edges of your garden to run wild.

Bloom times of pollinator-attracting plants

Spring:

- alder (pollen only)
- almond
- asparagus
- black locust
- blueberry
- borage
- cherry
- clover
- crocus
- dandelion
- henbit
- maple
- mustard
- peach
- plum
- poppy
- purple dead nettle
- radish
- rose
- rosemary
- serviceberry
- squill
- vetch
- willow

Summer:

- alfalfa
- basswood
- bee balm (and wild bergamot)
- blackberry
- borage
- buckwheat

- clover
- coneflower
- corn (pollen only)
- cosmos
- fireweed
- globe thistle
- hollyhock
- lavender
- Mexican sunflower
- milkweed
- mint
- mustard
- oregano
- partridge pea
- radish
- ragweed (pollen only)
- raspberry
- rose
- Russian sage
- sourwood
- stonecrop
- sumac
- sunflower
- sweet marjoram
- thyme
- tulip-tree
- vetch
- viper's bugloss
- virgin's bower
- yarrow

Autumn:

- aster
- boneset
- cosmos

Bee balm is one of the flowers we use to attract pollinators to our garden.

- fireweed
- goldenrod
- ironweed
- Joe Pye weed
- mountain mint
- smartweed
- sneezeweed
- stonecrop
- sunflower
- wingstem

The lists above suggest some plants that are particularly good for attracting pollinators, focusing on species that you may already have growing in or around your garden. When choosing pollinator plants, remember that showy, cultivated flowers (like irises and modern roses) have often been bred to reduce their output of pollen and nectar, so wildflowers or old-fashioned cultivated plants (like single-petaled roses) are a better bet for your pollinator garden. In addition, members of the carrot, mint, and aster families, with their many tiny flowers in each head, are particularly useful if you'd like to attract the smallest pollinators. You should aim to have at least three different

Some pollinators lay their eggs inside hollow stems, which the insects fill with food for their young before capping the ends with mud. You can make simple nest bundles for native bees by cutting bamboo of various diameters, making sure that one end is plugged by the node and that the other end is hollow. Hang your nest bundles horizontally under your eaves or in another dry spot, and the bees will lay eggs over the summer that will hatch in the spring.

In addition to needing flowers for nectar and requiring specific host plants for their caterpillars to eat, butterflies are attracted to sources of salt. These gaudy pollinators often congregate at the edges of drying puddles, on damp manure, or where humans and other animals have peed.

types of plants blooming in the spring, three in the summer, and three in the fall, and should be sure to cover the very early spring and late fall when pollinators are often in dire need of food.

Next, ensure that the wild pollinators have nesting sites available. Although you *can* build nest sites for pollinators, just letting the stems of plants like sunflowers and goldenrod stand through the winter will help out many species. Some pollinators need patches of bare soil, while yet others require a bit of nearby woodland. In general, letting the edges of your yard go wild will do much of the work of attracting native pollinators for you.

If you want to get a bit fancier, you can make a butterfly feeder . . . by peeing on the ground. Although nectar is a high-energy food source, the sweet liquid tends to lack salt, so butterflies and other nectar-eaters need to track down another source of this important nutrient. Male butterflies, in particular, spend a lot of time puddling—gathering around drying puddles or other sources of salt. Later, the males will pass a package of salt to the females as a gift when they mate.

Of course, as in the world of the soil, not all pollinators are purely allies of the garden. For example, the pollinator shown below is a fly that mimics a bee. Since the species appears so bee-like, the greater bee fly is able to get close to the burrows of solitary bees, into which it flings its eggs. When the bee fly eggs hatch out, the larval flies feed on the larval bees, often killing the latter. However, as with most parts of garden ecology, bee flies still have an important niche in the ecosystem—there's no balance without predators as well as prey.

The greater bee fly (*Bombylius major*) is a good pollinator, but the insect also parasitizes solitary bees and wasps.

Gardening with Beneficials in Texas

By Eric Paulus

A black swallowtail caterpillar munches on dill.

Photo credit: Sona Shah.

Providing a habitat for insects is my favorite part of gardening. At my current location, I'm a bit more than three years into creating an ecological balance. I garden commercially, but never use any "organic" sprays (no neem, Bt, etc.). I am absolutely seeing the benefits now: no major outbreaks as they are quickly mitigated.

(continued)

(continued)

Photo credit: Sona Shah.

Avoiding all chemicals, even organic ones, has promoted a healthy garden ecosystem on Eric's farm.

My favorite helper plants include yarrow, tansy, parsley, khella (*Ammi visnaga*), and cilantro for the little wasps and hoverflies. We use a borage hedge as a green lacewing nursery. Radish flowers, African blue basil, tusli, chamomiles, cornflowers, and any allium flowers also attract all sorts of life in the garden.

And, surprisingly to me, the absolute best is fennel. Every day, all day, the flowers are covered with the most diverse number of species, including literally dozens of varieties of wasps at one time.

(continued)

(continued)

Eric and his wife run a small urban farm in East Austin, Texas. To learn more, go to www.regenerationatx.com.

I know I'm forgetting many, but all these are great to include in the garden. It's also important to have various types of flowering plants throughout the year. For me, this means letting many naturally adapted plants (weeds) flower, especially in the winter.

Predators

Speaking of predators, the third group of wholly-positive invertebrates consists of the bugs who consume bad insects. Spiders, centipedes, dragonflies, mantids (a.k.a. praying mantises), ambush bugs, assassin bugs, lacewings, ladybird beetles (a.k.a. ladybugs), ground beetles, true wasps, digger wasps, hoverflies,

Photo credit: Brian Cooper.

Ladybugs are the classic garden predator. Brian Cooper attracts ladybugs early in the season by growing bachelor's buttons, and he finds that his efforts result in a healthy ladybug population for the rest of the year.

THE GARDEN ECOSYSTEM

and robber flies all subsist primarily or entirely on other insects during some stage of their life cycle.

Praying mantises eat both good and bad insects. It's handy to know what mantis egg cases look like so you can leave the spongy structures behind when pruning fruit trees.

Although many of the species listed previously are generalist predators, eating whatever ends up in front of them, all of these insects help keep pest population explosions in check. For example, I accidentally let the beetles on my green bean plants get out of control one summer, and soon thereafter I saw a pair of praying mantises move in to take advantage of the bounty. Sure, the mantises might have been eating butterflies yesterday, but I consider them beneficial insects because they eat at least as many bad bugs as good.

Another category of predators is the parasitoids. Braconid wasps, ichneumonid wasps, chalcid wasps, and parasitic flies all lay their eggs on other insects, and unlike true parasites, the wasps and flies eventually kill their hosts. That's great news in the garden since many of the prey insects are bad bugs, like tomato hornworms or bean beetles, so the parasitoids keep the pests under control. As a side note, in case you're scared of the term "wasp," all of the parasitic wasps are too small to sting human gardeners.

This hornworm is further along in the parasitization cycle than the one I pictured earlier. The caterpillar is dead in this photo and the wasps are getting ready to hatch out of their cocoons.

Many gardeners fall in love with the idea of predatory and parasitic insects and decide to buy some of these critters to seed their garden. However, I believe that you really need to encourage all of these species at the ecosystem level. I've heard of people opening a container of expensive insects, only to have them all fly away because the garden isn't a hospitable environment for the predators to live in.

Pediobius foveolatus wasps parasitize Mexican bean beetle larvae, but you have to buy these tropical wasps each year to protect your bean planting.

Instead of spending your money on insects, why not spend a bit of time encouraging the good bugs you already have to stick around and reproduce? Many predatory insects depend on flowers during some stage of their life cycle, so you can encourage them just like you did native pollinators by ensuring you have copious pollen and nectar sources available throughout the growing season.

In fact, you might receive double the benefit from any nest sites you put out for your native pollinators. Blog reader Brian Cooper erected mason-bee blocks in his garden, and ended up encouraging mud daubers by providing wet mud nearby.

Photo credit: Brian Cooper.

All of these caterpillars were collected by a mud dauber (*Sceliphron* sp.), which paralyzed the plump morsels and stashed them in the nest chamber along with an egg. The dauber's baby will feast on the caterpillars as it grows.

Dragonflies (and toads) need a small pond in which to lay their eggs.

Assassin bugs, like this immature wheel bug (*Arilus cristatus*), use their long mouthparts to suck other insects dry.

Brian wrote: "When we went to harvest the bees, we found mud daubers also laid eggs in some of the unused cells. They collect food for their young inside the cell before they cap it with mud. I found one cell that was filled with caterpillars and a dauber larvae, and another cell with a pupa of the mud dauber and just bug parts left over."

Weedy edges will also encourage predatory insects since the predators need to be able to find lots of insects to eat even when your garden pests are under control. In addition, dragonflies need a pond into which they can lay their eggs, and many insects will benefit from having a very shallow body of water from which they can drink. In general, when attracting predatory insects, it's imperative not to use any pesticides (even organic ones) and to allow low levels of pest insects to fly under your radar. If there aren't any bad bugs around, your predatory insects won't have anything to eat and will go somewhere else.

In fact, you've probably sensed a theme throughout this chapter. To encourage the good bugs, let nature move into your garden. Leave things alone and the beneficials will come.

Attracting Predators with Weeds

BY ROBERTA WALKER

Photo credit: Albert Reavis.

Roberta Walker shows off a day's harvest in September 2013.

Here in our corner of Northwest Missouri, we are fortunate enough to have a large population of Chinese mantids (*Tenodera aridifolia sinensis*). Come mid-summer, I can hardly take a step through the garden without spotting one!

Also abundant in our area, however, is the very destructive and dreaded squash bug. I'm sure most readers of this book can relate to this nuisance in the garden. It is my belief that our population of

(continued)

(continued)

Photo credit: Albert Reavis.

Praying mantises keep squash bugs in check.

mantids is the primary reason I am even able to harvest squashes and pumpkins, or even cucumbers and melons (since the squash bugs are nondiscriminating).

I understand that mantids can also be somewhat relentless in their hunt for food, preying upon another generally popular "good bug," the ladybug. And so I take some extra measures to keep these two garden helpers apart.

Because I am recruiting the mantids primarily to hunt down my squash bugs, I am sure to leave tall, woody-stemmed weeds (mostly giant ragweed) on the north side of my squash and cucurbit patches. Mantids enjoy skulking about these weeds in their off time, searching for mates and a place to establish oothecas (egg sacks).

For the ladybugs, I plant dill and coriander along the edge of a hardy, wild patch of Queen Anne's lace. In my experience, these plants tend to attract ladybugs. It's also no coincidence that I choose to plant my peas near this "ladybug patch" to keep my aphid population in check.

(continued)

(continued)

In addition to providing a mantis habitat, ragweed is also an excellent pollen source for honeybees and wild pollinators. However, allergy sufferers will prefer to cut the plants down before they bloom.

I know for some this seems a disastrous approach to pest management. Leave such heavy-seeding weeds right next to the garden? Well, yes! Much like Anna (in fact, largely because of Anna), I enjoy the no-hassle method of drowning my weeds away with kill mulches. So whenever I feel as if these patches are beginning to intrude on garden territory, I simply break out the cardboard and voila! Not only do I put the weeds back in their place, but I add just a tad more fertility to my beds as well.

Deer are one of the few vertebrates with no redeeming value in the garden.

Chapter 4:
Helpers with Backbone

The previous chapter may have made it sound like good bugs are the holy grail of bad-bug control. However, it also helps to pay attention to the wider ecosystem when managing populations of pest insects. Even though you may not realize it, your bug problem might have actually started with a decision to eradicate snakes from your orchard or turtles from your tomato patch. So I'll spend a bit of time answering the question: which vertebrates are friends and foes in the garden?

Mammals

I'm going to skim over large mammals since most people are familiar with these creatures and will soon learn which ones are helpful or problematic in the garden. Here in southwest Virginia, deer are our worst large-mammal problem, but bloggers in South Africa report monkeys tearing apart their gardens, wild boars root up Japanese gardens, and parrots (instead of mammals) wing in to eat Australian gardens to the ground. Among slightly smaller American mammals, woodchucks (a.k.a. groundhogs) and rabbits are also problematic garden browsers, while skunks are mostly beneficial (although they can root up the garden inappropriately while trying to find their favorite foods: beetle grubs and cutworm larvae). In general, I suspect most of us would prefer that all large mammals steer clear of our gardens.

Then there are the small mammals, which mostly consist of little critters that look like mice to the untrained eye. Small mammals can be good, bad, or neutral in the garden, so it's handy to know which animal is which.

Voles are mice relatives that tunnel through the garden, gnawing on potatoes and carrots, eating the bark around the base of young fruit trees, and generally making trouble. You can tell voles from other small mammals by their rounded bodies, long fur, small ears, and short tails. We've found that a good dog and cat provide quality vole control in the garden, although you may have to put up with churned earth where your dog obsessively chased the vole back along its underground tunnel.

Shrews and moles are often blamed for the damage done by voles, but these species are insectivores and live almost entirely by eating both good critters (like earthworms) and bad critters (like slugs) in your soil. Shrews can be distinguished from voles by the fact that their ears are concealed by fur and their teeth are often stained brown. Moles are larger, with long-nailed, paddle-like front feet used for digging, and with eyes and ears concealed by fur. Mole tunnels are another giveaway that you're dealing with insectivores— in addition to the

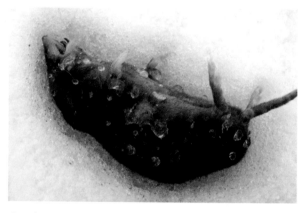

This shrew, caught by our dog, was once a beneficial part of the garden ecosystem.

shallow runways that voles also create, moles excavate deeper tunnels, then mound the earth on the surface a bit like crayfish do. Unless you're trying to create a perfectly flat lawn, you should be happy when you see signs of shrews and moles since the insectivorous mammals prove that your soil ecosystem is in balance. You can encourage shrews and moles in the same way you encourage smaller soil workers—by feeding the soil with rich organic matter but otherwise leaving the earth alone.

The last type of small mammal you may notice in the garden is bats. These aerial predators eat large quantities of flying insects, so they can make their hunting grounds more habitable to humans. Bats don't have much impact on the garden itself, though, so I'll leave you to research more about these fascinating furry fliers on your own.

Phoebes are common predators of garden insects.

Birds

Like small mammals, birds can be either good or bad in the garden. Despite stories about crows digging up sprouting corn kernels and cardinals eating the fruits from berry bushes, most birds we see in our garden seem to act as beneficial predators near the top of the garden food chain—in other words, they're eating insects. *Edible Forest Gardens: Volume 2*, by Dave Jacke, lists the following birds as particularly beneficial in the garden for their insect-consumption skills: swifts, woodpeckers, flycatchers (including the phoebe, which is a common garden resident in the eastern United States), vireos, chickadees, titmice, nuthatches, brown creepers, wrens, bluebirds, wood warblers, tanagers, and orioles. As an added bonus, I've noticed that birds enjoy perching on stakes and trellises in the garden, depositing their manure around the bases of the plants below.

Woodpeckers deserve a special mention since they seem to be good friends of fruit trees. In *Organic Orcharding*, Gene Logsdon reports that promoting woodpeckers by leaving natural woodland adjacent to your orchard can reduce overwintering codling moth larvae by 52 percent, and one of my readers emailed to say that woodpeckers in his yard were eating borers in his apple trees. Like several other types of birds, woodpeckers are cavity nesters, so they can be encouraged with appropriate birdhouses, or by leaving standing-dead trees outside your garden perimeter.

This downy woodpecker is pecking apart a praying-mantis egg case, but woodpeckers are also prone to eat borers and codling-moth larvae on fruit trees.

Whole books exist on the topic of encouraging birds in your garden, but the gist usually boils down to providing them with a nesting habitat, with protective cover (bushes, hedges, or brush piles), and with food. I'll just add two brief notes that are of particular interest for gardeners hoping to attract insect-eating birds to their yards. First, man-made houses are especially handy for cavity-nesters like bluebirds, since you can make the entrance hole just the right size to attract the species you're looking for. And, second, birdseed isn't the right feeding solution for many of the bug eaters—instead, you'll want to allow prey insects to live at low levels just like you did to promote predatory insects.

Reptiles

Like most of their relatives, fence lizards are insect eaters.

Anoles are common garden-dwelling lizards in the southeastern United States.

Lizards, like birds, are generally friends of the garden. Large lizards in other parts of the world (such as iguanas) may consume plants, but the little lizards most of us are familiar with prefer eating insects, spiders, centipedes, snails, other lizards, and young mice. You can encourage these beneficial reptiles by providing small crevices in which lizards can hide. Rock piles and dry-stone walls are good shelters for lizards, and we've noticed that skinks (a type of lizard) particularly enjoy hiding out between logs in our woodshed.

People tend to be afraid of snakes, but many of these slender creatures are actually vital parts of the garden ecosystem, acting as predators of worms and other ground-dwelling invertebrates and (in some cases)

The eastern worm snake spends much of its time underground hunting earthworms. The snake also looks very much like a large worm when you dig it up.

loosening the soil as they burrow through the earth. My stance on snakes is very similar to my stance on garden insects—I know how to identify the poisonous snakes that live in my area, and then I assume that every other snake I see is good. Here in southwest Virginia, only rattlesnakes and copperheads have dangerous bites, and both are rare in the garden.

How do you encourage beneficial snakes like the ones shown in this chapter? Blog reader Brian Cooper wrote in to say: "A couple years ago, I started lining my garden beds with logs from fallen tree branches (~6" in diameter) to allow for some moisture retention and to keep mulch in the beds while defining the paths. What I did not realize was that I was making a perfect home for earth snakes. This year, for the first time, I saw one while I was digging out our swale paths and accidentally disturbed one of these edge logs. These snakes are reported to eat arthropods and slugs, like to live underground, and can be found under logs." Other ways to encourage snakes include making rock or wood piles as you would for lizards, providing brushy cover as you would for birds, and leaving the ground alone as you would for soil workers.

Worms make up 80 percent of an average garter snake's diet.

Although they *will* take a bite out of your tomatoes, box turtles are generally friends of the garden since they love to eat snails and slugs.

Box turtles lay their eggs in loose soil, especially in the rotting wood of hugelkultur mounds. Once we started adding wood to our forest garden, baby box turtles turned up year after year.

While snakes and lizards are nearly all allies of the garden, I'd have to say that box turtles (the most common turtle found in gardens in the eastern United States) are neutral. Box turtles have a tendency to visit tomato patches, where they take one bite out of each ripe fruit, which can drive some gardeners crazy. Carry the turtles away, and they'll slowly but surely walk back to your garden and continue eating those tomatoes, and then they'll head over to clean up the dropped berries under your raspberry plants. On the other hand, if you can handle a few nibbles on your fruits, box turtles will pay their way by consuming large quantities of problematic snails and slugs (as well as friendly earthworms), so I enjoy seeing these shelled reptiles in my garden. Box turtles move into the same kinds of environments that snakes and lizards enjoy, but turtles are particularly sensitive to chemical use.

Amphibians

Gardeners may have mixed feelings about reptiles, but amphibians are usually welcomed with open arms. And with reason—frogs and toads live entirely on invertebrates like insects, spiders, centipedes, millipedes, snails, and earthworms. To attract toads, many books recommend making houses out of upturned flowerpots with a door broken out of one side, but I've found that these warty amphibians prefer hanging out under the mulch in my vegetable garden instead. Toads became even more plentiful in my yard after I installed a small water garden, and the warty amphibians love spending time under a wooden pallet that my husband tossed down on swampy ground beside one miniature pond.

If you live outside North America, chances are you're unfamiliar with salamanders, and even many residents of the United States confuse these amphibians with lizards. Their scale-less, moist skin, though, is a dead giveaway that salamanders are relatives of frogs and toads, and that they depend on moisture of the surrounding environment to stay alive. If you maintain a heavy mulch in your garden, you may soon find mole salamanders (along with toads) moving in to eat your insects, worms, snails, and slugs.

Blog reader Jackie Wilson emailed to tell me that, in her Pacific Northwest garden, "the slug problem was insane" until

Toads hide under mulch during the day and come out at night or during rains to hunt garden slugs.

she started encouraging salamanders and toads with "little ponds in tall grasses, large damp compost piles with lots of coarse vegetable matter (like corn stalks and twigs), [and] rotting-log-lined berry beds . . . The little ponds I refer to are simply the biggest

Mole salamanders spend most of their life in the earth.

plant-pot saucers I can find, with a couple of flattish stones placed to make sure the critters can get in and out easily, next to an overturned container of some sort for snug cover. These are located in out-of-the-way wildish areas, which describes about two-thirds of the perimeter of my garden . . . Love those amphibians, and they are much lower maintenance than ducks."

Farm Animals

Speaking of ducks, if you mention insect control to ten permaculturalists, at least nine will tell you to invest in these aquatic poultry. Others sing the praises of chickens, guineas, and muscovies, while geese are recommended as weeders of your garden. The idea is to utilize stacking—a central permaculture tenet—to gain multiple yields from the same garden space, all while letting your livestock do some of the farming work for you.

We don't let our chickens run freely through the garden, but we do use the poultry to turn pest insects like Japanese beetles and cicadas into nutritious eggs.

Poultry *do* have a lot of potential in the garden, but you'll find that it requires more effort to incorporate livestock into your garden than to simply encourage existing wildlife to do the same job. The trouble is that all poultry will eat (or mash down or scratch up) your garden plants if they're not managed carefully. That caveat aside, if you're going to raise poultry anyway, why not find a way to get them to eat some bad bugs in the garden too?

A chicken tractor is a great way to utilize chickens in the garden without letting your vegetables suffer from the birds' destructive habits.

We've had the most extensive experience with chickens, which we consider great friends for cleaning up weeds and soil insects on fallow ground. Chicken tractors are a handy way to keep your chickens in one small area so they don't toss around mulch, demolish tomatoes, and scratch up seedlings throughout the garden, and you can also let chickens run free in a summer-only garden during the cold season when nothing is growing. Harvey Ussery suggests that bantams may be a slightly better choice than standard-size chickens when free ranging in active gardens since bantams don't scratch as much, but any chicken is going to be a problem in an active vegetable garden. In an orchard or other perennial planting, though, chickens may be just what you need for insect control, as long as you ensure the birds have enough space so that they don't over-fertilize your plants.

Unlike chickens, which can provide eggs and meat, guineas are usually just raised for meat (or for eye candy). In the garden, guinea fowl are handy since they're reputed to control squash bugs, ticks, grasshoppers, and snails. I haven't heard from anyone who free ranges guineas in their vegetable gardens, but I suspect there would be similar caveats to those mentioned about ducks below.

So that brings us to the permaculture darling—ducks. I'll admit up front that my personal experience with ducks is only one month old at the time of this writing, but many premier permaculturalists have shared their extensive wisdom on the topic. First of all, there's the potential for effective pest control—ducks adore slugs, insects, and worms, while muscovies (a type of duck) are even known to hunt down flies. Meanwhile, the same ducks produce delicious and nutritious eggs and meat for their human keepers. However, as one of our blog readers reported, "[Ducks] are very destructive in the veg garden. We fence them out of the veg garden completely."

Carol Deppe, author of *The Resilient Gardener*, is perhaps the most experienced duck-keeper in permaculture circles today. She loves ducks for their ability to control slugs in her Pacific Northwest garden, but she warns that waterfowl eat most garden plants. Unlike chickens, ducks don't scratch, but their big feet do crush tender plants, their wet manure makes vegetables much less appealing, and their voracious appetite means they eat up everything in sight.

How does Deppe work around these duck foibles? She fences ducks into areas just beyond the garden, where their droppings attract slugs that are promptly snapped up by the poultry. Deppe raises Ancona ducks and reports that the fowl can be kept in by fences as low as two feet high, provided that the ducks have plenty of food and water and aren't separated from their friends.

Ducks hunt through mulch with their bills rather than with their feet, so they tend to do less damage than chickens do. On the other hand, the waterfowl will eat most plants, so they can't be left in a vegetable garden unattended.

Carol Deppe also lets ducks forage through her garden at intervals when she's standing by to keep an eye on them. She reports that ducks prefer insects and slugs over other food choices, so the birds will eat the pests first before chowing down on your tomatoes. However, you'll want to protect seedlings and low-growing greens before letting ducks into the garden for even these short field trips.

As appealing as it may be to imagine that poultry will take care of pest insects, the truth is that if you really care about your garden, all livestock will need to be fenced out of your vegetables most of the time. That's why I primarily focus on ecosystem-based pest-control techniques in this book. While you have to monitor ducks as they hunt slugs in your garden, no one has ever complained about the actions of a toad.

Scratching Up Codling Moths

Dave Miller tosses sunflower seeds under his apple trees in the winter to tempt wildlife to scratch up codling-moth larvae.

Blog reader Dave Miller, who lives in Washington State near Portland, Oregon, uses wild birds and other critters to keep codling moths to a minimum. "I don't have any chickens or other permaculture animals—instead I try to use wild animals for those things," Dave explained.

In his area, codling moths are a "horrendous pest." Although putting a nylon stocking over each young fruit has achieved some success in the past, Dave notes that "those are a lot of work." This year, Dave's trying something new—a daily dose of sunflower seeds tossed around the base of each of his apple trees over the winter.

"Here is my logic with that," Dave wrote. "Codling moths overwinter as larvae in bark crevices or in the leaf litter under the tree. I noticed that when I throw birdseed on the ground, the birds' natural instinct is to scratch the ground, even though the seed is sitting on top of the soil. When I throw birdseed under my apple trees, the birds happily scratch away for hours. I theorize that during the winter, if a bird uncovers a larva, the bird will gobble it up. Even if the birds don't eat the larvae, the insects will be exposed to the elements, which will probably make the insects unhappy and might even kill them."

(continued)

(continued)

Photo credit: Dave Miller.

Nylon stockings act as a physical barrier, preventing codling moths and other problematic insects from laying their eggs in young fruits.

In addition to the towhees and other birds that visit Dave's orchard feeding station, he notes that a second shift comes by at night, including squirrels, rabbits, raccoons, and opossums. The mammals and birds deposit manure at the same time they scratch up the ground, so their actions do double duty to help the trees.

Will Dave's codling moth pressure be lower this year because of his bird-feeding campaign? The jury's still out, but I wanted to share this innovative technique with you anyway so you can experiment with the idea in your own garden. Maybe you can find a way to lure skunks to your lawn when Japanese beetle grubs are close to the surface, or perhaps you can bring gnatcatchers to your peaches just as the Oriental fruit fly larvae emerge. Get creative and you could be encouraging wild animals to do the garden pest-control work for you!

THE GARDEN ECOSYSTEM

65

PART 2

Controlling Pests

Japanese beetles are one of the insects I control by handpicking.

Digger wasps are supposed to prey on Japanese beetles, but we see few digger wasps and lots of beetles in my garden.

Chapter 5:
Letting Nature Take
Its Course

Now that you understand the basics of ecosystem-level bug management, the rest of this book will cover specific forms of pest control that a gardener might utilize, such as succession planting and trap crops. But I wanted to start by telling you about a much less hands-on method than the aforementioned examples. In fact, my own first line of defense when a bad bug shows up in my garden generally consists of waiting and hoping.

Asparagus beetles defoliated my asparagus plantings during our first couple of gardening years.

The theory underlying this strategy is that nearly every pest insect has several predators just waiting to eat the bad guy up. But the predators don't have any reason to head to your yard until the pest insects reach a certain level—who wants to comb through an entire orchard in search of one colony of aphids? As a result, you sometimes have to hold onto your temper and let pest-insect populations reach critical mass in hopes of attracting their predators.

I didn't know what I was seeing when the first asparagus beetle eggs and larvae showed up on my plants.

My experience with asparagus beetles taught me the importance of this often-overlooked pest-insect remedy. I used to think of asparagus as a vegetable that required no maintenance, so I wasn't terribly concerned when I first saw tiny grubs nibbling on my asparagus leaves. But within a couple of weeks, entire plants were defoliated! Research suggested my garden was suffering from an infestation of asparagus beetles, which lay their eggs in lines along asparagus fronds, with the eggs then hatching into voracious caterpillar-like grubs. Asparagus beetles can go through several generations per year, so if you don't take action and the beetles have no predators, large plantings of asparagus can be killed back to the ground. That means you won't be eating many spears next spring.

Traditional asparagus-beetle control consists of spraying Bt, but I'm leery of that method since Bt is a relatively broad-spectrum insecticide (even if it is based on a bacterium). So, during the first year of our infestation, I handpicked. (More on handpicking in Chapter 8.) This was a particularly difficult project since asparagus fronds are tender and you really have to squish beetle eggs to kill them, plus it's hard to find the grubs and eggs amid all that greenery. To cut a long story short, the beetles won round one.

However, the next year I knew what I was looking for and I instituted early-and-often handpicking. That fall, I cut down all of the dead fronds and raked up the mulch, adding the debris to the chicken coop for our flock to pick over. It also helped that I started to squish the asparagus beetles immediately upon their arrival that year, so my harvests broke the earliest cycles of asparagus beetles' egg laying.

But the tides didn't really turn until predatory stink bugs moved in. During the height of the asparagus-beetle infestation, I noticed the first of these beneficial insects dining, but one bug wasn't able to make much of a dent in the beetle population. However, by the next year, the tables had turned, and there were enough stink bugs and few enough beetles that the former were able to keep the latter in check. Recently, my only nod toward asparagus-beetle control has been to squash one or two adult beetles and perhaps ten eggs in the spring, then to step back and let the predatory stink bugs do the rest of the work.

Which brings me back to the moral of the story. If I had sprayed Bt when the infestation began, the asparagus-beetle population wouldn't have built up to the point that predatory stink bugs would

A predatory stink bug has impaled an asparagus-beetle grub on its long snout.

have come to call. And the chemical may also have harmed the nearby beneficial insects, so it's possible that there wouldn't have been any predatory stink bugs around to hunt down the beetles that survived. This is the primary reason I eschew chemicals (even organic ones) in the garden. Sometimes, doing nothing will yield much better long-term effects . . . as long as you can hold onto your temper in the meantime.

Natural Plant Defenses

Slightly holey plants still produce copious Brussels sprouts, which may be tastier and more nutritious due to the insect damage.

Imagine a caterpillar hatching out of its egg and beginning to munch on a Brussels sprout leaf. Most gardeners think that the Brussels sprout is defenseless unless a helping hand comes along to squash that marauder. The plant knows better. As soon as juices in the caterpillar's mouth interact with the open wound on the plant leaf, the Brussels sprout realizes that there are herbivores in the area. Immediately, the plant releases a chemical into the air that attracts parasitoid wasps. The wasps hone in on the plant-produced scent, then lay their eggs in the caterpillar's body, eating the caterpillar alive from the inside out.

Scientists are just beginning to understand the vast array of natural defenses that plants use to fend off insects when gardeners aren't around to step in. Only a few instances of plants attracting predatory insects are known so far, but many vegetables create herbivore-unfriendly chemicals in their leaves as soon as a caterpillar, aphid, or other insect begins to chow down. The chemicals are costly for the plants to produce, slowing down both growth and fruit ripening, but the compounds are worth it since they kill or damage the nibbling insects and let the wounded plant bounce back.

Plants are also willing to alert their neighbors about insect problems, with the result that an entire planting block can become resistant after an herbivore has nibbled on a single plant. Plants communicate by emitting chemicals into the air, passing cues through roots and mycorrhizal connections, and possibly even by

(continued)

(continued)

making sounds. In all of these cases, the neighboring plants respond by beefing up their own defenses so that herbivores will have to look elsewhere for a snack.

What does all of this mean for the gardener? First of all, low levels of bad insects should probably be left alone since their presence will help plants protect themselves from other herbivores in the neighborhood. But you might also be interested to learn that many of the chemicals that fruits and vegetables use to keep away herbivores are the same chemicals that make for a healthy human diet. For example, cabbages build antioxidants into their leaves to keep away pests, and those same antioxidants help prevent cancer in people who eat those leaves. I wouldn't be surprised if the deeply delicious flavors of organic vegetables are also the result of compounds created by plants for the purpose of keeping bugs at bay. Yet another reason to let nature take its course . . . within reason.

Chapter 6:
Timing Plantings to
Bypass Bugs

The ecosystem-level approach to insect control that I explained previously is the best long-term solution to bug problems in the garden. But the technique can feel painfully slow as you wait for your garden to come into balance. How do gardeners manage in the meantime?

If a little bit of benign neglect doesn't do the trick, I turn to timing my plantings to avoid the worst insect problems. I mentioned in Chapter 2 how I use timing to keep cabbageworm problems to a minimum, by planting early in the spring and late in the fall when the butterflies aren't out and about. I'll regale you with two more examples of how to use planting time to outwit pests.

Squash Vine Borers

Our first approach to squash-vine-borer control was spraying Bt. Visit the glossary for more information about this and other chemicals mentioned in the text.

Squash vine borers were my arch nemesis during our early years on the farm, so much so that I even resorted to spraying Bt on the plants' stems. (Okay, pictures don't lie—I made my husband do the spraying.) And I'm glad to say that the Bt *didn't* help. Why am I glad? Because if that seemingly innocuous spray had proven effective, I might never have figured out less intrusive ways to keep vine borers in check.

Variety selection was part of my solution, as I'll explain in the next chapter, but the biggest reason I started being able to harvest summer squash is because I learned to succession plant these speedy vegetables biweekly in the summer garden. Here in zone 6 (last frost: May 15, first frost: October 10), I plant crookneck (summer) squash on May 1 (a gamble), May 15, June 1, June 15, and July 1 (a slight gamble), a schedule that allows us to be overwhelmed with tasty squashes despite heavy vine-borer pressure and without the use of other control measures beyond variety selection.

Yes, the bad bugs move in and kill our squash plants eventually, but not until after I've collected at least one big harvest from each bed. By the time the earliest vines start failing, I have another planting of summer squash just waiting to take their place, and I can rip out the infected plants and put the debris in the chicken coop so my garden doesn't turn into a breeding ground for vine borers.

I highly recommend this method to all organic growers battling vine borers, but northern growers should take special notice. In their colder climate, vine borers have only a single generation per year, meaning that if these gardeners wait to plant their squash until after the vine borers lay their eggs, late plantings of squash will be pristine.

Succession planting is handy with other types of vegetables as well, although the strategy only works if you choose varieties that put out a big harvest right away. For example, I succession plant bush beans rather than growing runner beans since the former provide lots of green beans before the bean beetles move in to dine, and I also succession plant cucumbers in order to beat cucumber beetles and bacterial wilt. On the other hand, succession planting wouldn't be a good choice for tomatoes since even determinate varieties require months of growth before they ripen their first fruit.

Another benefit of succession planting comes when the food reaches our table. A few studies have suggested that cucurbits (and perhaps other vegetables) have more micronutrients on hand when they mature their first fruits, so the earliest harvest often tastes best. Some gourmet farmers pull out their squash vines after the first picking as a matter of course, figuring it's better to maximize flavor rather than yield. So maybe the borers are trying to do us a favor by prompting us to eat the most nutrient-rich and tasty vegetables possible.

Cicadas

I learned my next lesson on timing the hard way. In 2012, periodic cicadas crawled out of the ground in our area and regaled us with their ocean-like symphony. I was intrigued by the natural occurrence and enjoyed feeding these protein-rich insects to our chickens, so at first I thought the periodic cicadas were a boon to our farm. Then I saw the damage pictured to the right.

It turns out that cicadas lay their eggs in tender twigs of young trees, and seem to preferentially choose fruiting species over wild saplings. When the young cicadas hatch from their twig homes, the nymphs drop to the ground and tunnel down to feed on the tree's roots. While the root sucking may be a long-term problem, the real issue is that the nymphs damage fruit-tree twigs so much while coming out of their eggs that the branches often break off and die.

Female cicadas lay their eggs on the twigs of young fruit trees, creating extensive scars.

Brian Cooper shared these photos of cicada killer wasps "taking cicadas right out of the air."

Of course, even cicadas have natural predators, but the insects' periodic nature is designed to keep predation to a minimum. Cicada killers and other animals that preferentially feed on cicadas can only survive at low population levels most of the time since their food is scarce. Every 13 to 17 years, the adult periodic cicadas come out of the ground and provide a feast, but by then, the predator levels are so low that the majority of the cicadas survive untouched. That's why we have to get a bit wilier when dealing with these insects—periodic cicadas have outwitted their natural enemies and we can't count on help from nature.

The short-term solution to cicada damage is to net adult cicadas away from the twigs as soon as you hear periodic cicadas calling. But smarter orchardists also plan around cicada cycles. If you go online to the Magicicada Database[1] run by the University of Connecticut, you can choose your state and county and then find out when periodic cicadas have recently emerged in your region. Add the appropriate number of years to those emergence dates and you'll know when the next brood will be out looking for baby fruit trees.

In a perfect world, you'd plant fruit trees no more than two years before cicada-emergence dates since cicadas aren't as interested in older trees. Smart orchardists also choose not to winter prune fruit trees during a year when periodic cicadas are due to emerge, knowing the cicadas will do some of the pruning job for them. That's true permaculture gardening at work!

---

[1] http://hydrodictyon.eeb.uconn.edu/projects/cicada/databases/magicicada/ magi_search.php

Japanese beetles enjoy eating the leaves of French hybrid grapes.

Chapter 7:
Helping Plants
Resist Insects

In addition to timing, variety selection, row covers, companion planting, and proper plant nutrition can all go a long way toward reducing insect pressure in the garden. In fact, choosing resistant fruit and vegetable varieties is my favorite low-work method of insect control in our own garden.

Resistant Varieties

American grapes have thicker leaves with whitened undersides and tend to be less favored by hungry Japanese beetles.

Japanese beetles taught me my first lesson about variety selection. We had a terrible problem with these invasive beetles on our grapevines until I realized that French-hybrid grapes are much tastier to Japanese beetles than are American varieties. The latter can be distinguished by their thicker leaves, which are often whitened underneath, and by the relative paucity of beetles chowing down on the leaves. In addition to grapes, Japanese beetles also defoliated our young sweet-cherry tree, but damage on other plants seemed to stay at low enough levels that the trees could shrug it off. After switching our small vineyard over to American grapes and removing our cherry tree, the Japanese beetle pressure was reduced to the point where handpicking was sufficient to keep beetles at bay.

In general, variety selection can be a helpful strategy in controlling at least five of the dirty-dozen worst garden pests in the United States. The table on the next page includes pest-resistant varieties drawn from several different extension-service websites and other sources.

Cabbage varieties with dark green leaves are usually the most resistant to cabbageworms.

Insect-resistant vegetable varieties

Pest insect	Insect-resistant varieties
Cabbageworms	Collards, Brussels sprouts, broccoli, and cabbage are tastier to these insects than are other crucifers. Within each type of vegetable, vegetables with dark green, glossy leaves are more resistant to cabbageworms, while cabbage butterflies sometimes avoid laying eggs on red cabbage varieties. Resistant cabbage varieties include Chieftan Savoy, Early Globe, Mommoth, Red Acre, Red Rock, Round Dutch, and Savoy Perfection Drumhead.
Corn earworms	Any corn with a tight husk will be more resistant to earworms. Specifically resistant varieties include Country Gentlemen, Golden Security, Seneca, Silvergent, and Staygold.
Cucumber beetles	In general, cucumber beetles prefer zucchini-type squash over others and don't like burpless cucumbers as well as other varieties. Ashley, Chipper, Gemini, Piccadilly, Poinsett, and Stono cucumbers; Blue Hubbard, Early Prolific, Scallop, Straightneck, and White Bush squash; and Galia, Passport, Pulsar, Rising Star, and Super Star melons are all reported to be resistant to cucumber beetles. However, the more important issue is to select a variety resistant to the bacterial wilt carried by cucumber beetles. These wilt-resistant varieties include Connecticut Yellow Field, Harvest Moon, and Howden pumpkins; Waltham butternut; Buttercup squash; Black Beauty zucchini; and Ashley, Chinese Long, Chipper, County Fair, Eversweet, Gemini, Improved Long Green, Saticoy Hybrid, Sunnybrook, and Tokio Long cucumbers. Most watermelon varieties are resistant to bacterial wilt.
Squash bugs	Squash bugs prefer yellow summer squash over zucchinis, squash over pumpkins, pumpkins over gourds, and gourds over melons. Resistant varieties include acorn squash, butternuts, Early Summer Crookneck, Green Striped Cushaw, Improved Green Hubbard, Spaghetti, Sweet Cheese, and zucchinis (except for the susceptible Cocozelle).
Squash vine borers	Varieties resistant to squash vine borers tend to have thin, tough stems. In addition, vining types are more resistant than bush types since the former can root along their nodes and thus survive moderate levels of borer damage. The most resistant varieties include butternuts and Green Striped Cushaw, followed by Dickenson Pumpkin and Summer Crookneck. Other varieties reputed to have at least some resistance include acorn squash, Cucuzzi (also known as snake gourd), and Connecticut Field, Dickenson, and Small Summer pumpkins.

She also enjoys writing about her adventures, both on her blog at WaldenEffect.org, and in her books. Her first paperback, *The Weekend Homesteader*, helped thousands of homesteaders-to-be find ways to fit their dreams into the hours left over from a full-time job. In addition, a heaping handful of e-books serve a similar purpose.

Index

Flea beetles aren't a major problem on most vegetables, but they do tend to kill eggplants in our area.

Row Covers

Of course, if you don't plant cucurbits, you won't have to deal with squash vine borers, cucumber beetles, and squash bugs at all. While that's generally not my preferred approach to insect control, I have been known to avoid planting a vegetable species entirely due to insect pressure. For example, eggplants aren't our favorite vegetables, and in our area the plants are defoliated by flea beetles in short order. Rather than hunting for a solution to the flea beetle problem, we just skip growing eggplants and focus our energy on vegetables that we think taste better and that are easier to handle.

What would I have done if eggplants were my favorite food? In that case, I would have mimicked the effects of planting a resistant variety by growing the vegetables under row covers. These sheets of thin fabric let light, air, and water through while keeping insects out.

When using row covers to exclude pest insects, it's essential that you find a way to weigh down all edges of the fabric, and that you cover the plants at the seedling stage so no pest insects will find their way inside the protected tent. Some pests, like flea beetles and cucumber beetles, spend part of their life cycle in the soil, so you'll need to use proper crop rotation to ensure the pupae aren't already in your soil before you put a row cover in place—otherwise you'll be trapping the pest insects in with your plants rather than blocking the bugs out.

In addition to making sure your row cover does its job, you'll have to work around some of the negative aspects of this pest-control technique. All row covers block some light and rain, and even if you use the thinnest type of fabric, you should definitely keep a close eye on the moisture levels of soil under row covers. In addition, if you're growing vegetables like squash that require pollination, you'll either have to remove the row covers once the plants begin to bloom, or you'll need to hand-pollinate. As you can tell, row covers add another level of complexity to vegetable gardening, but they *can* provide a chemical-free pest solution if all else fails.

Hoverflies like this one are attracted to nectar sources in the garden, and their larvae stick around to eat aphids and caterpillars.

Companion Planting

Companion planting is a bit like choosing resistant vegetable varieties, but you instead plant the varieties you want and then cozy up a more toxic (from an insect's point of view) plant beside your favored crop. For example, some gardeners believe that interplanting basil with tomatoes will keep hornworms at bay. My experience with companion planting has been largely negative since I find that plants need to be very close together to get any insect-repelling effect, and then you see competition between the vegetable you're trying to grow and its companion.

Agricultural scientists agree that most companion planting isn't going to provide any pest-control help for the backyard gardener. However, a few interplanting mixtures seem to work. Trap crops (as I'll discuss in Chapter 8) can be used to draw insect pests away from your main crop, and flowers near your vegetables will definitely attract beneficial insects. (See Chapter 3 for suggestions on which flowers to plant.) In addition, the roots of African and French marigolds have been shown to emit a chemical that repels nematodes (a type of microorganism that can harm roots), although you'll get the most bang for your buck by planting marigolds as a cover crop that is killed shortly before planting your nematode-sensitive crop. Finally, at least one source suggests that corn planted amid your squash plants may confuse squash vine borers looking for a spot to lay their eggs.

Although I pooh-pooh most types of companion planting, I do feel that a diverse garden will fare much better than a monoculture when treated organically. On my own homestead, I break the ground up into permanent beds about three feet wide and anywhere from five to twenty feet long. Except for corn (which has to be grown in large blocks for wind-pollination purposes), I plant each type of vegetable in several different places around the garden, so a bed of cucumbers might be surrounded by beans, tomatoes, and Swiss chard rather than by the other cucumbers I'm growing that year. This patchwork-quilt garden gives me

A diverse garden attracts pollinators and confuses pests.

many of the benefits of companion planting without requiring the extra work of dealing with species mixtures all in the same bed. (On the downside, my technique does make planning the garden rotation more complicated, but they say puzzles are good for fending off Alzheimer's, right?)

Plant Nutrition

The last facet of outwitting insects is to make your garden less susceptible to insect infestations by keeping your plants healthy. I already touched on this issue briefly in Chapter 2 when I mentioned that many aphid problems can be traced back to over-fertilization of the plants being consumed. A related problem occurs with green beans—bean beetles can't digest the form of nitrogen created by bacteria in nitrogen-fixing nodules in the plants' roots, but the beetles love the form of nitrogen that the plants suck up directly from compost (or from other fertilizers) in the soil. So one way to keep bean beetles in check is to skip

If you keep the nitrogen levels in your soil low, you won't see many Mexican bean beetles. Instead, minor pests like this broad-headed bug (*Alydus eurinus*) will show up to suck juices out of the seeds.

top-dressing any garden area where you plan to grow beans that year, forcing the plants to create all of their own nitrogen from scratch.

On a related note, many organic gardeners will tell you that every insect infestation is linked to a nutritional deficiency in the plant. While this idea has intuitive appeal, I've yet to find any solid data to back the hypothesis up. On the other hand, a well-nourished plant is likely to provide more nutrient-dense food for the table, so there's no reason not to provide the best possible nutrition for your vegetables. Applying organic amendments like compost and mulch will probably do the job for you, especially if you mix things up and draw your organic matter from different sources each year. If you want to be scientific, a soil test is a good way to get a handle on any potential deficiencies, at which point you can apply rock dusts or other amendments to boost mineral levels into the recommended range.

Keeping the soil balanced and plants healthy is something I do as a matter of course, but there are times when I put more energy into the campaign than usual. If a new insect problem pops up and doesn't respond to any of my usual control techniques, that's a good time to start researching nutrient deficiencies. I was tipped off to the bean problem mentioned earlier because many of my bean beds were overrun with beetles, but the beans I'd planted into not-very-decomposed rye stubble were virtually untouched. The rye stubble was locking up nitrogen from the compost I'd applied to the soil, which in turn required the bean plants to kick their rhizobial bacteria into gear to create homegrown nitrogen for the plant. If you keep your eyes open for similar scenarios in which one bed of a vegetable is untouched while its neighbors are overrun, you'll soon discover which deficiencies or excesses may be at work in your own garden.

If you catch them early, tent caterpillars are easy to handpick. Initially, you can greatly reduce tent-caterpillar populations by removing egg cases while pruning your fruit trees over the winter.

Chapter 8:
Handpicking

After tent-caterpillar eggs hatch, the cobwebby homes of the larvae are also easy to pull out of low branches.

I hope the previous chapters didn't make you think that keeping bad bugs in check is as simple as sitting on the porch and watching the good bugs and other wildlife eat them up. Sure, some of that happens, but there are times when the gardener needs to step in and keep things in line. When that time comes, my main defense is handpicking.

How to Pick Bugs

I deter imminent population explosions in my garden primarily through handpicking. While this sounds like I've retreated to the Dark Ages, I assure you that I can hit all of the problematic spots in my acre-plus garden in less than ten minutes on a summer day. The trick is to pick during the cool of the morning so that the insects can't easily fly away, to pick often (three times a week is the minimum), and to know which problematic insects are likely to be where when. It's also handy to understand that beetles tend to drop directly down when startled, so if you put a cup of water under their resting place, you can "pick" these fliers without touching anything with your bare hands.

Various sources will tell you to knock bad insects into a container of soapy water or gasoline, but I use plain water in a straight-sided cup or jar. The insects almost never clamber back out, and by keeping my liquid additive-free, I can dump the whole thing into the chicken coop, turning bad bugs into free eggs. Japanese beetles (and the occasional June bug) are the primary insects I treat this way since they're the ones our chickens will peck up before they fly away. Other bugs I often handpick include asparagus beetles (which I addressed in more detail in Chapter 5), bean beetles (which I merely squish between my fingers since the chickens won't eat them), cabbageworms (which I squish or feed to the chickens, depending on my mood), and tent caterpillars. Dave Miller, who shared his codling-moth-deterrent strategy in Chapter 4, adds slugs to his handpicking campaign, snipping the slimy nibblers in half with scissors. In general, if you're fast enough to catch them, all pest insects can be handpicked.

Picking by the Calendar

In all cases, it's important to start picking when pest populations are low if you want to make a difference. I find it handy to mark on my calendar when major infestations (like Japanese beetles) are likely to arise so that I can nip them in the bud. The earliest Japanese beetles to emerge from the soil emit pheromones that attract other beetles, so if you catch the first beetles to congregate on your beloved plants and remove them, chances are the biggest party will set up shop in the weeds instead of in your berry patch.

Even for insects that don't congregate in this manner, once you kill a large portion of the first insects to show up in the spring, each early-bird then won't be able to reproduce and turn into twenty or a hundred pest insects later that summer. That's why it might be worth pulling out plantings (like buggy beans) on which the pests have reached critical mass in the interest of keeping pest populations low throughout the garden. And that's also why it's so important to handpick with regularity, since daily (or at least thrice-weekly) pickings will keep insect populations at a dull roar.

Trap Crops

Some gardeners take the handpicking strategy to another level by growing trap crops—plants that the pest insects prefer over the variety you want to harvest. In large fields, your best bet is to plant a row of the trap crop in a rectangle completely surrounding the plants to be harvested since this buffer can prevent pest insects from making their way into the heart of the commercial planting. In contrast, on the backyard scale, your goal should simply be for the trap crop to be located in close proximity to the planting you want to protect.

When using trap crops, you'll need to keep a close eye on the trap planting and to handpick the pest insects there as soon as they appear. Otherwise, the trap can become a reservoir of bad bugs that will spread into the rest of your garden, making the trap much less of a boon to your crops.

What should you plant as a trap crop? Bug attractants can be as simple as an early planting of the same variety you want to grow for your main crop, or they can be a tastier (from an insect's point of view) variety that you plant beside the main crop. The table on the next page suggests several proven trap-crop varieties you might want to try in your own garden.

Plants used as trap crops

Pest to be attracted	Trap crops
cabbage root flies	Chinese cabbage, collards, and radishes
cabbageworms	collards
carrot root flies	garlic, medic, onions
Colorado potato beetles	horseradish, Superior potatoes (and pre-sprouted potatoes of other varieties that will come up before the main crop), tansy, Vittoria eggplant
cucumber beetles	Baby Blue Hubbard squash, nasturtiums, and New England Hubbard squash
flea beetles	Chinese cabbage, collards, nasturtiums, radishes, Vittoria eggplant
harlequin bugs	Southern Giant Curled mustard
Japanese beetles	*Pelargonium × hortorum* geraniums. (Unlike other trap crops, these geraniums not only attract Japanese beetles, they also paralyze and kill the pests.)
leaf-footed beetles	sorghum variety NK300 and Peredovik-type sunflowers
pepper maggot flies	hot cherry peppers
slugs	chervil, French marigolds, and sorrel
squash vine borers	nasturtiums
stink bugs	black-eyed peas, buckwheat, millet, sesbania, sorghum, sunflowers, and triticale
tomato hornworms	dill and lovage

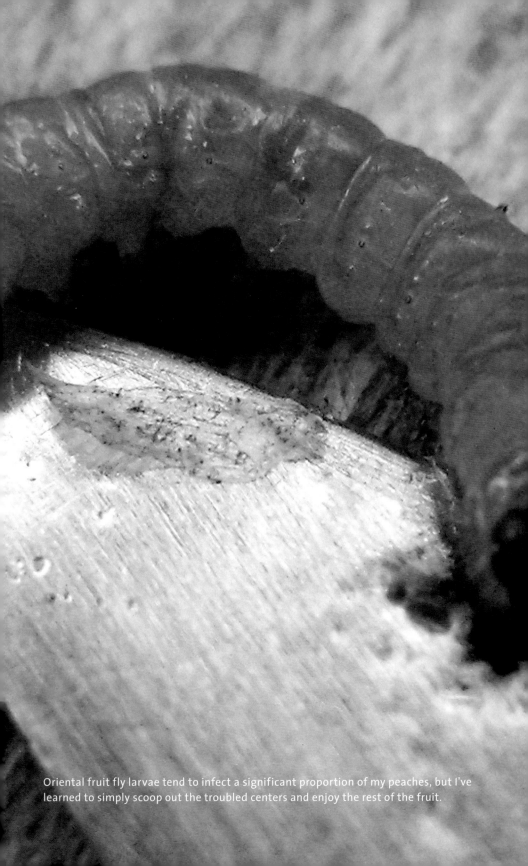

Oriental fruit fly larvae tend to infect a significant proportion of my peaches, but I've learned to simply scoop out the troubled centers and enjoy the rest of the fruit.

Chapter 9:
Changing Your Mind-Set

So you've boosted your beneficials and tried to outwit the bad bugs that remain, but your corn still has an occasional earworm and your apples are adorned with spots. What can you do?

Eat the produce anyway! In *Organic Orcharding*, Gene Logsdon suggests that we lower our expectations for homegrown fruit before we resort to spraying. He figures that if a third of his apples are only fit to give to the hogs, that's okay—the fruits will be turned into bacon. Another third might need to be cut up for cooking into applesauce and baking into pies—who doesn't like apple pie? That leaves a third of his crop that is unblemished and beautiful, perfect for storing in a root cellar and nibbling on all winter.

In contrast to Logsdon's realistic approach to blemishes, most Americans have grown up eating grocery-store produce, all of which was sprayed with something (be it organic or not) to keep pest damage to a minimum. Next, up to 20 percent of those fruits and vegetables were discarded for cosmetic reasons before the most beautiful specimens made their way to the supermarket.

With all of this work to give the consumer perfect-looking fruits and vegetables, it's no wonder that many modern Americans now turn up their noses at twisted or insect-nibbled cucumbers from their own gardens. But if you learn to cut out a bad spot here and there, you'll soon discover that the ugliest tomatoes really can be the tastiest ones, and that some trees seem to concentrate more flavor in the bug-nibbled fruits. Once you find yourself going out of your way to choose the uglier apple, knowing it will taste better, then you've truly become a permaculture gardener.

Acknowledgments

This book wouldn't have reached your hands without the help of many people, each of whom deserves a huge thank-you. Readers of my blog always get top billing because their enthusiasm for homesteading topics (and willingness to share their experiences) is what keeps me writing. Specifically, Brian Cooper, Roberta Walker, Jackie Wilson, Dave Miller, Herrick Kimball, and Eric Paulus emailed me tips that ended up within these pages, and dozens of commenters on the blog helped me see the garden ecosystem from a broader perspective. I hope you'll join this vibrant community by visiting www.WaldenEffect.org.

Family and friends provided the next level of support for the book while it was a work-in-progress. My parents, Adrianne and Errol Hess, each read early drafts, then they both pushed my paperbacks on unsuspecting friends at farmer's markets, herbariums, and more. My husband, Mark Hamilton, took several of the photos that appear within these pages, and he also did the difficult job of helping me carve time out of our busy homesteading schedule to write. Moral support and other intangible aid came from a slew of people, including Wendy Jehanara Tremayne (author of *The Good Life Lab*), Rose Nell Hamilton and Jayne Wead (the best in-laws ever), Kayla Scarberry-Jacobs (my favorite fan and garden helper), and Frank Hoyt Taylor (movie-star neighbor extraordinaire). Closer to home, my two spoiled cats made the huge sacrifice of sharing my lap with a computer, during which time the felines were forced to seek my divided attention one cat at a time.

Next, I would be remiss if I didn't thank Skyhorse Publishing, and specifically my editor Jenn McCartney, for being willing to bend their rules to match my homesteading-style of publishing. Without Skyhorse's help, this book would be far less beautiful and accessible to you, the reader.

Last, but surely not least, thank *you* for reading! I hope *The Naturally Bug-Free Garden* hit the spot and that your garden this year is a more vibrant, healthy ecosystem because of what you read within these pages. If you reach for your camera instead of for the Bt the next time a pest insect comes to call, then my journey to share natural pest-control techniques with you will have been entirely worth it.

Resources

Books

Cranshaw, Whitney. 2004. *Garden-Insects of North America*. Princeton, NJ: Princeton University Press. With hundreds of photos, this is my favorite text for garden insect identification.

Deppe, Carol. 2010. *The Resilient Gardener*. White River Junction, VT: Chelsea Green Publishing. If you'd like to learn more about using ducks in the garden, this book should be your first stop.

Jacke, Dave, and Eric Toensmeier. 2005. *Edible Forest Gardens*. White River Junction, VT: Chelsea Green Publishing. This two-volume set is still the best source for in-depth information about combining trees with other plants to mimic wild ecosystems. I recommend the books here primarily for the extensive appendices located in the second volume, which include a list of plants that provide shelter and food for beneficials, a bloom-time calendar of nectar-producing flowers, and ecosystem information for beneficial vertebrates and invertebrates.

Hess, Anna. 2012. *The Weekend Homesteader*. New York: Skyhorse Publishing. My previous book will help you get started on creating a no-till garden and planning crop rotation.

Kimball, Herrick. 2013. *The Planet Whizbang Idea Book for Gardners*. Moravia, NY: Planet Whizbang. This home-published book includes several easy remedies for battling invertebrate pests.

Logsdon, Gene. 1981. *Organic Orcharding*. Emmaus, PA: Rodale Press. Although an older book (and currently out of print), Logsdon's text is full of tips you won't find in more modern libraries. As the title suggests, *Organic Orcharding* focuses on growing fruit and nut trees without the use of harmful chemicals.

Nardi, James B. 2007. *Life in the Soil*. Chicago: University of Chicago Press. Beautiful line drawings and an engaging text introduce the life history of many common soil vertebrates and invertebrates.

Phillips, Michael. 2011. *The Holistic Orchard*. White River Junction, VT: Chelsea Green Publishing. If you'd like to learn more about controlling pest insects (and diseases) on fruit, this book should be your first stop. Michael Phillips's *The Apple Grower* is also recommended for pome-specific information.

Ussery, Harvey. 2011. *The Small-Scale Poultry Flock*. White River Junction, VT: Chelsea Green Publishing. Ussery's book includes information on turning chickens into a working part of your garden, along with a rundown on niches of other types of poultry.

Xerces Society. 2011. *Attracting Native Pollinators*. North Adams, MA: Storey Publishing. As the title suggests, this beautifully illustrated book will help gardeners create a nesting and feeding habitat for bees and other wild pollinators.

Websites

The Agricultural Extension Service (www.csrees.usda.gov/Extension/) is the best identification option for gardeners who prefer to capture their unknown insects and bring them to a real person to ID. In addition, each state's extension service website is a great source of specific information relevant to your location.

Bug Guide (bugguide.net) is a great resource since the site's volunteers are usually glad to identify invertebrates from photos.

Magicicada Database (hydrodictyon.eeb.uconn.edu/projects/cicada/databases/magicicada/magi_search.php) will help you learn when periodic cicadas are due to emerge from the soil in your location.

Worst Garden Pests by Region (www.motherearthnews.com/organic-gardening/worst-garden-pests-by-region.aspx) is the result of a *Mother Earth News* survey of 1,300 gardeners.

Walden Effect (www.waldeneffect.org) is my personal blog, where my husband and I post daily updates about happenings on our homestead.

Glossary

APIARY: a collection of honeybee hives.

BENEFICIAL: good. In this book, I use the term to refer to animals that help maintain the overall health of your garden.

BEER TRAP: a method of capturing slugs by setting a shallow dish of beer on the ground in the garden. Slugs crawl inside and drown overnight.

BT: *Baccillus thuringiensis.* This soil-dwelling bacterium is often used as an organic pesticide. However, Bt kills a wide range of insects (which can include flies, mosquitoes, beetles, nematodes, and caterpillars of moths and butterflies), so the pesticide will harm some beneficials. In addition, Bt has been shown to have some small toxicity to humans and to the environment. Common trade names include DiPel and Thuricide.

BORER: various types of insects that chew into the roots and trunks of trees or other plants.

CATERPILLAR: a larval moth or butterfly.

CAVITY NESTER: an animal that lays its eggs and raises its young in holes in trees.

CHEMICAL FERTILIZER: fertilizers are added to the soil to provide nutrients for plants, the most notable of these nutrients being nitrogen, phosphorous, and potassium. Chemical fertilizers are man-made compounds in which the nutrients are supplied in their raw chemical form rather than bound to organic matter.

Carolina wrens are an example of cavity nesters, willing to lay their eggs in holes in trees, or in discarded flowerpots and unused mailboxes.

CHICKEN TRACTOR: a small pen for poultry that includes both the roosting area and an outdoor run. Chicken tractors are usually highly portable so they can be moved to a new spot every day.

CODLING MOTH: *Cydia pomonella.* An insect whose larvae feed on apples, pears, and English walnuts.

COMPETITION: among plants, competition usually involves individuals struggling to get more resources, such as light, nutrients, and water. Plants that are forced to compete with others may grow hardier, but seldom produce as much food.

COMPOST: decomposed organic matter that is often used to fertilize organic gardens.

COVER CROP: a plant grown to add fertility to a garden. For more information, see my e-book *Homegrown Humus*.

CRUCIFER: a member of the plant family Brassicaceae. Common garden crucifers include broccoli, Brussels sprouts, cabbage, cauliflower, collards, kale, mustard, radishes, and turnips.

CUCURBIT: a member of the plant family Cucurbitaceae. Common garden cucurbits include cucumbers, gourds, melons, pumpkins, and squash.

CULTIVATING SOIL: digging in the earth, usually with the purpose of controlling weeds or loosening hard ground. In the home garden, examples would include running a rototiller between rows to suppress weeds or using a hoe to kill weed seedlings. On a larger scale, cultivating can mean plowing before planting and churning up the soil between rows after planting.

DECOMPOSER: any organism that breaks down dead plants and animals into soil.

DEFOLIATE: to remove leaves. When involving insects, defoliation usually means that the animals are eating the leaves.

DETERMINATE TOMATO: a variety in which the fruits all ripen close to the same time.

DIATOMACEOUS EARTH: a crumbly soil made from fossilized diatoms that once lived in rivers, lakes, and oceans. Diatomaceous earth is often used as an organic pesticide because the substance irritates insects' exoskeletons and absorbs important oils, causing the insects to dry out and die. Diatomaceous earth only affects insects when the compound is dry, so it quickly becomes neutralized by rain and doesn't cause environmental problems. However, diatomaceous earth can irritate the skin, lungs, and eyes of people, and the dry compound is a broad-spectrum insecticide that will kill most invertebrates in its path.

DISPERSE SEEDS: moving seeds from one spot to another. Many plants count on animals to disperse their seeds.

ECOSYSTEM: a community of interacting plants and animals.

EGG CASE: the structure that surrounds and protects eggs.

FALLOW: part of a garden that is not being used to grow food at the current time.

FERTILIZATION: adding nutrients to the soil, often in the form of compost, manure, chemical fertilizers, compost tea, or urine.

GENERALIST PREDATOR: an organism that will eat many kinds of animals rather than just one type.

A wolf spider is an example of a generalist predator since the spider will eat any small insect it can catch.

GRUB: a larval beetle.

HARDY PLANT: a plant that is able to survive cold or other difficult conditions.

HERBIVORE: an animal that eats plants.

HUGELKULTUR: a method of adding rotting wood to a garden to increase the organic matter content of the soil. The wood is usually buried in the ground.

INSECTICIDAL SOAP: a special kind of soap sprayed on plants to kill insects. Insecticidal soaps work by disrupting the insects' cell membranes. Although considered organic, insecticidal soaps are broad-spectrum insecticides that kill most soft-bodied insects upon contact.

INVERTEBRATE: animals without a backbone.

IRON-PHOSPHATE BAIT: a type of purchased poison used to kill slugs and snails. Trade names include Sluggo and Escar-Go.

LARVA: an active, immature form of an insect, such as a caterpillar or a grub.

LEAFY GREENS: vegetables in which the leaves are eaten. Common examples of leafy greens include kale, mustard, Swiss chard, and collards.

MICRONUTRIENT: a mineral that plants require but only use in very small amounts. The eight main micronutrients are boron, chlorine, cobalt, copper, iron, manganese, molybdenum, and zinc.

MONOCULTURE: a large planting of a single crop. For example, a five-acre cornfield.

MULCH: a substance (usually plant matter) laid on the surface of garden soil to hold in moisture, prevent weed germination, and increase organic matter content of the earth.

MYCORRHIZAL FUNGI: beneficial fungi that team up with plant roots, capturing minerals from deep in the soil and trading those nutrients for sugars provided by plants.

NEEM OIL: oil pressed from the fruit and seeds of an evergreen tree, *Azadirachta indica*. Neem oil is used as an organic pesticide, but the oil is a broad-spectrum chemical that will kill most insects that the substance comes in contact with.

NEMATODE: a very small kind of worm. Some nematodes harm plant roots.

NEST SITE: a spot where an animal lays its eggs.

NO-TILL: a method of gardening that strives not to disturb the soil. Commercial-scale no-till farmers often use toxic herbicides to kill weeds in lieu of plowing, but no-till gardeners simply lay down heavy mulches and hand-weed.

NUTRIENTS: minerals and other substances that plants and animals need.

ORGANIC MATTER: dead plants and animals and their waste products, which are applied to soil as fertilizers or mulches. Garden examples include manure, compost, leaves, and straw. The dark-colored humus found in soil is also referred to as organic matter.

PERMACULTURE: sustainable farming systems. Because the term "organic" has become industrialized in recent decades, gardeners who are more serious about growing food in harmony with the earth replaced the term "organic" with the term "permaculture."

PESTICIDE: a chemical that kills insects.

PHEROMONE: a chemical emitted by an animal to communicate with other animals.

Butterflies bring beauty to the garden but are inefficient pollinators compared to wild and cultivated bees.

POLLINATION: fertilizing a potential fruit by transferring pollen from one flower to another or by transferring pollen from one part of a flower to another part of that flower.

PREDATOR: an animal that eats other animals.

PUPA: the intermediate form between a larva and an adult insect. Pupae are often protected inside cocoons.

ORGANIC GARDENING: growing plants using only natural inputs. The definition of "natural" varies greatly, and some amendments that are allowed by current organic standards can be harmful to the environment.

RHIZOBIAL BACTERIA: microorganisms that live within the root nodules of legumes. Rhizobial bacteria take nitrogen out of the air, converting the nutrient into a form that plants can use.

ROCK DUST: finely crushed stones used to supply minerals to garden soil.

ROTATION: growing different types of vegetables in different parts of the garden each year. See *The Weekend Homesteader* for more information. Garden rotation can lower pest and disease levels.

ROW COVER: a thin fabric laid over garden plants that lets air, light, and water through. Row covers keep pests out and can help protect plants from frost.

SOLITARY BEES: bees that don't live in colonies. Examples include mason bees, sweat bees, and carpenter bees. Honeybees are *not* a solitary bee since many individuals work together in one hive.

SPINOSAD: an insecticide based on the bacterium *Saccharopolyspora spinosa*. Spinosad is a broad-spectrum insecticide that will kill most insects on contact.

STICKY TRAP: a method of capturing pest insects after attracting them to a certain color or odor. Sticky traps kill insects by gluing the invertebrates to the surface of the sticky trap, similar to the way flypaper works.

STUBBLE: the roots and lower stems left behind in a field when a crop is mown down.

TILL: to churn up the earth, usually with a plow or rototiller.

TOPDRESS: to add compost to the surface of soil, usually as a fertilizer.

WEEDY EDGE: part of the garden left alone to revert to wild plants.

About the Author

Anna Hess dreamed about moving back to the land ever since her parents dragged her off their family farm at the age of eight. She worked as a field biologist and nonprofit organizer before acquiring fifty-eight acres and a husband, then quit her job to homestead full time. She admits that real farm life involves a lot more hard work than her childhood memories entailed, but the reality is much more fulfilling and she loves pigging out on sun-warmed strawberries and experimenting with no-till gardening, mushroom propagation, and chicken pasturing.